MA BANDE DESSINÉE

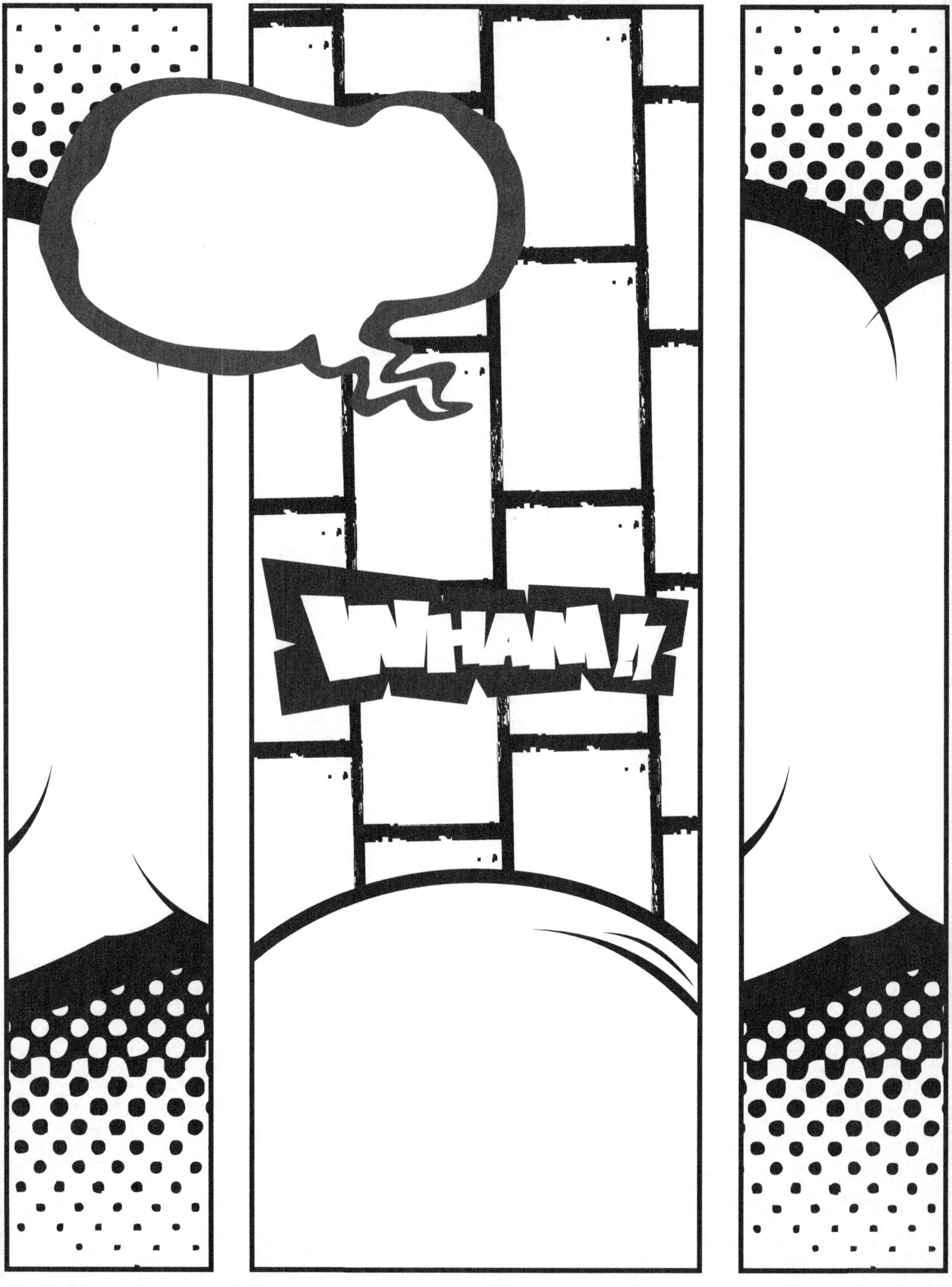
WHAM!

HUH?!
CRAAAAAAACCK

CRAAAAAAACCK

POW POW

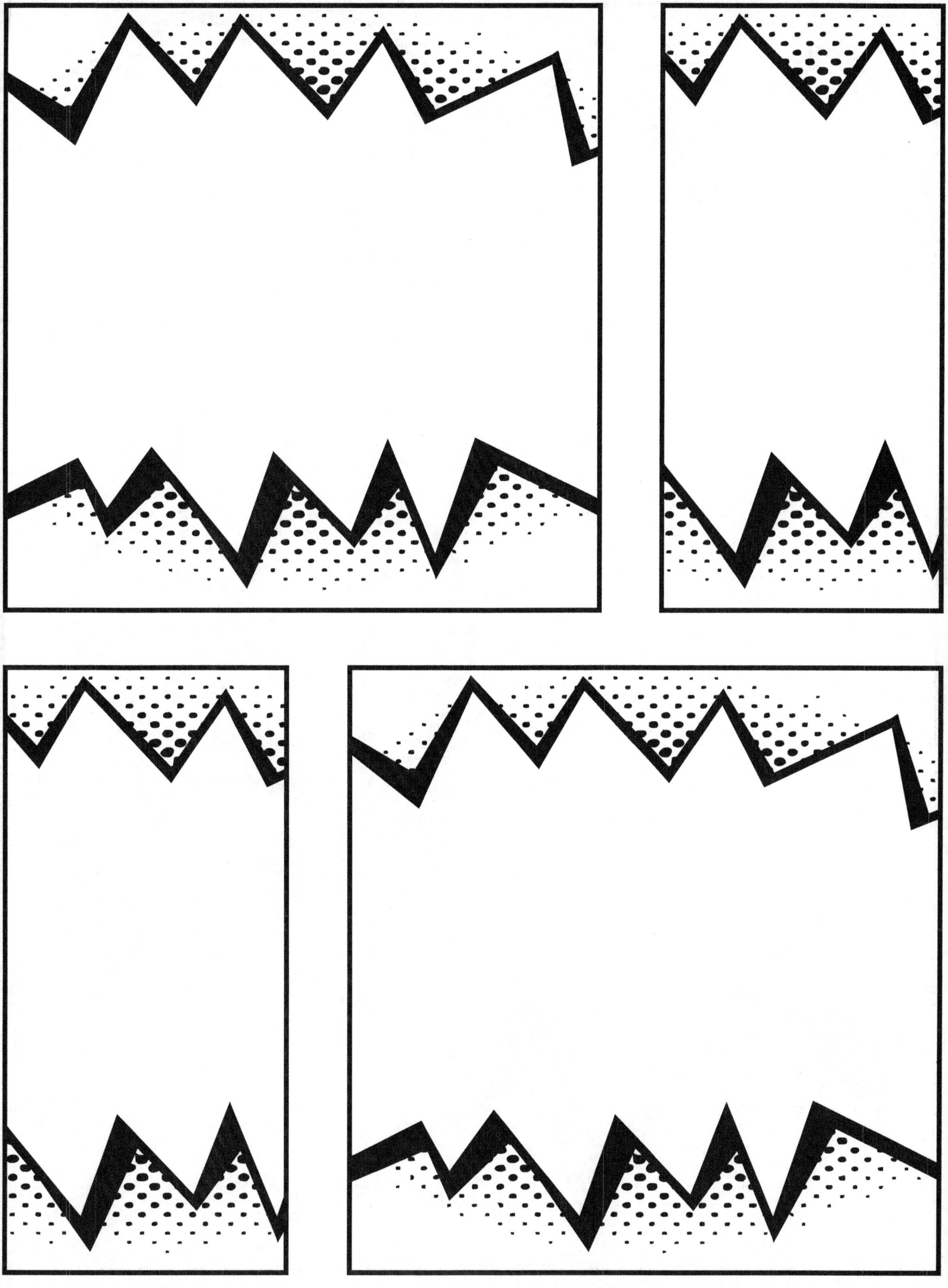

BOOM

HUH?!

HA! HA! HA!

CRASH!

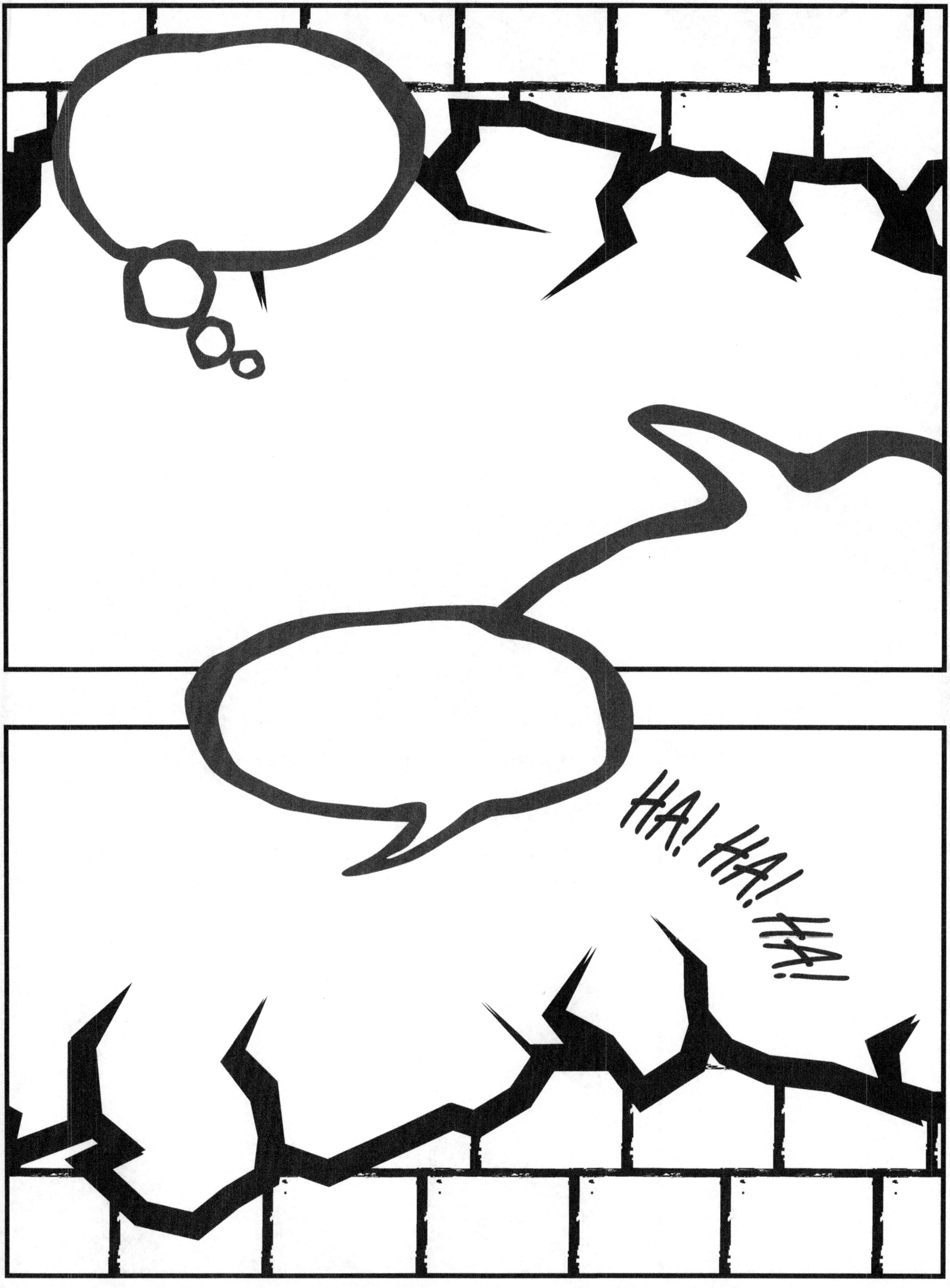
HA! HA! HA!

SPLAT!!

OUCH

BAM

BAM

WOW

Pow Pow

BOOM

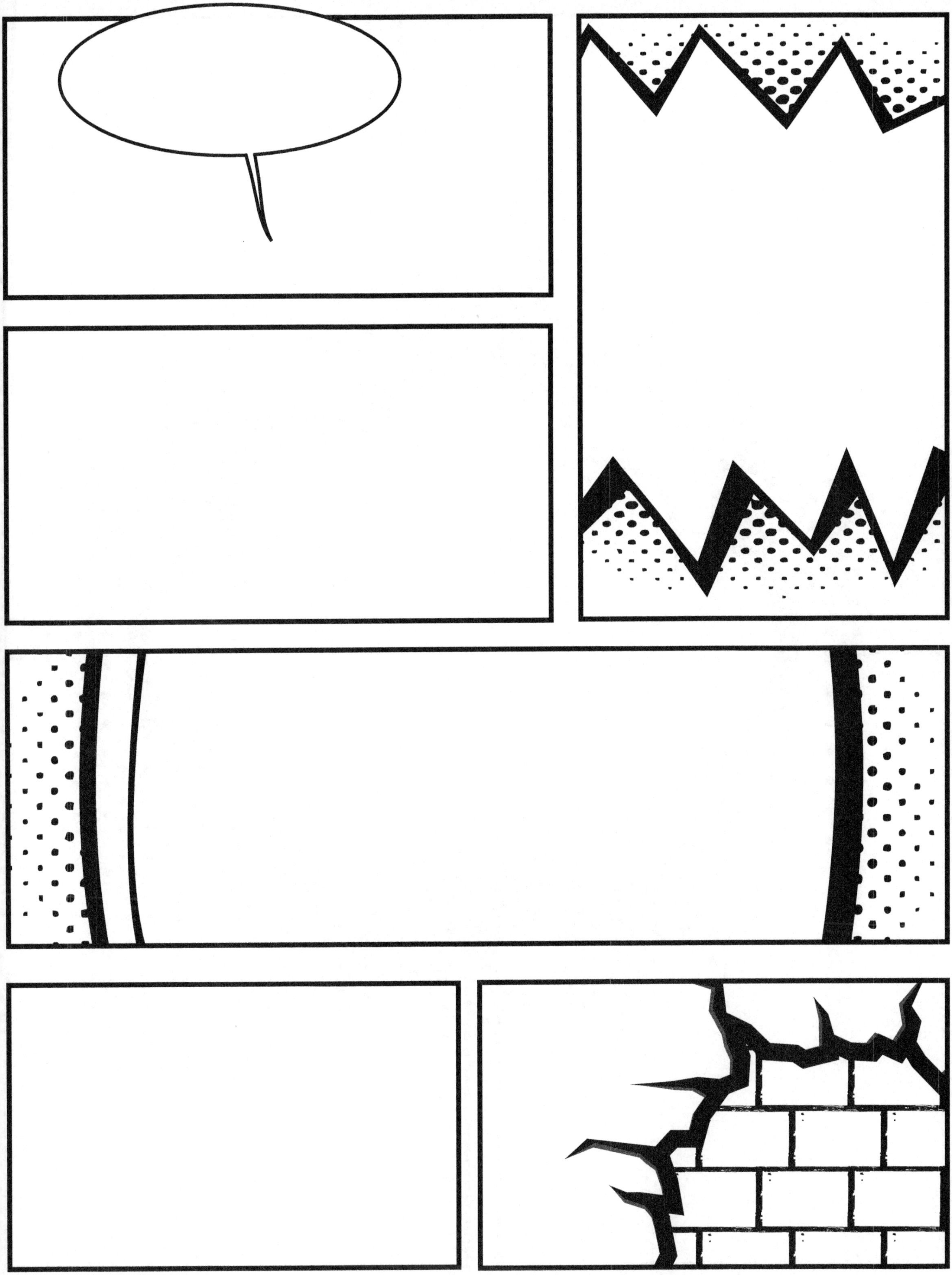

Boooooooooom

BAM!

CRASH

WHAP!

CRUNCH!!!

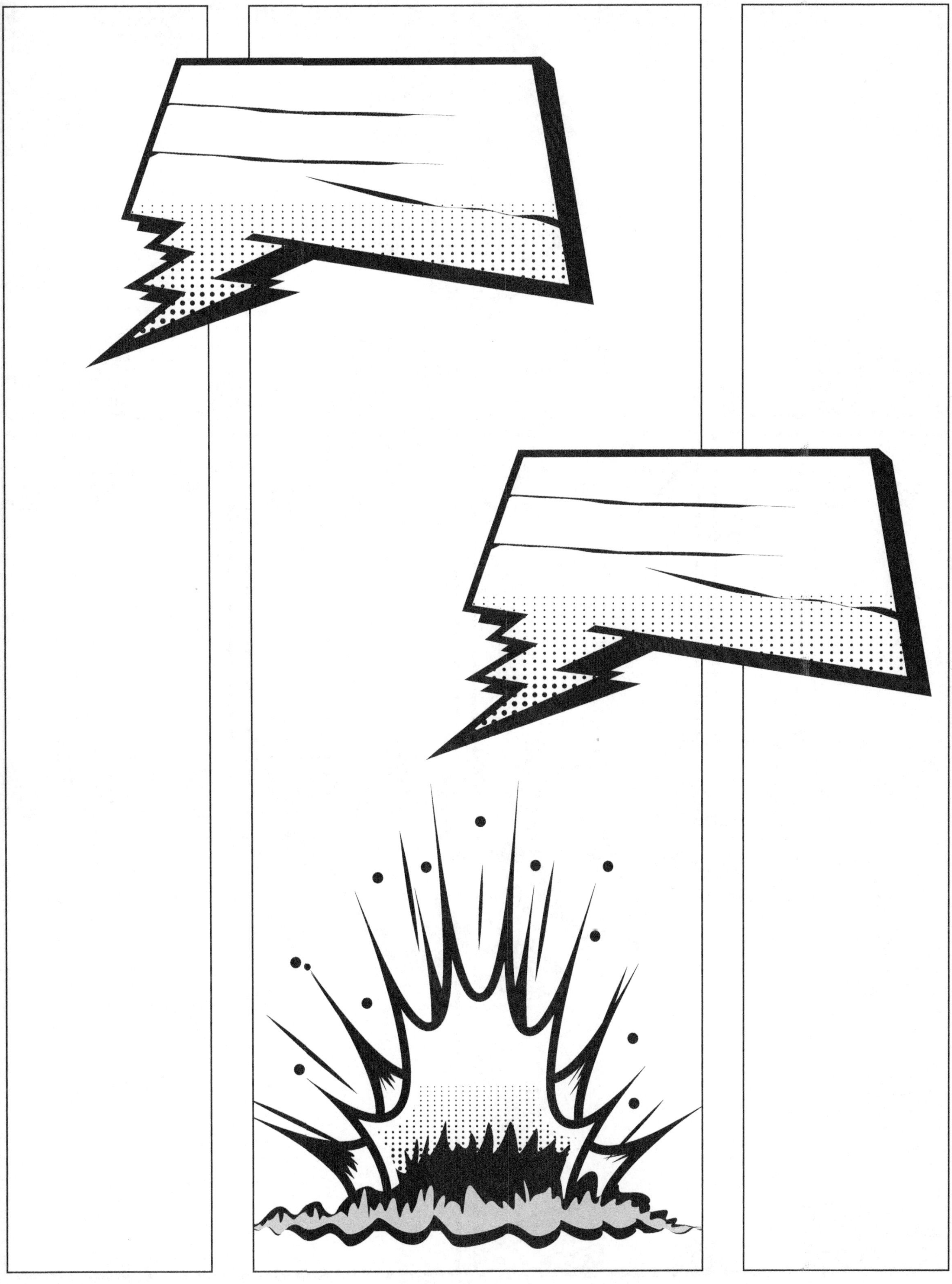

POW

BOOM

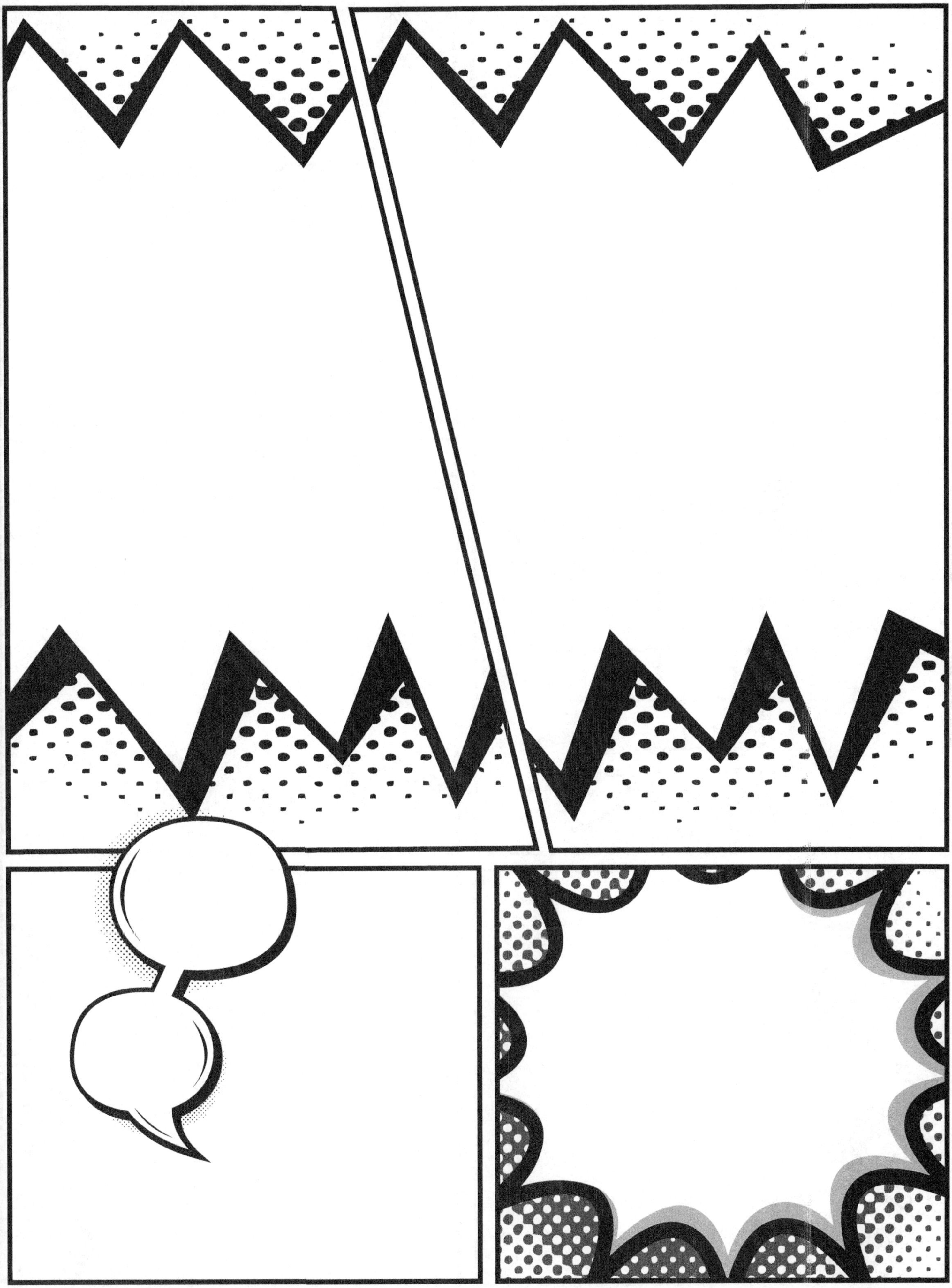

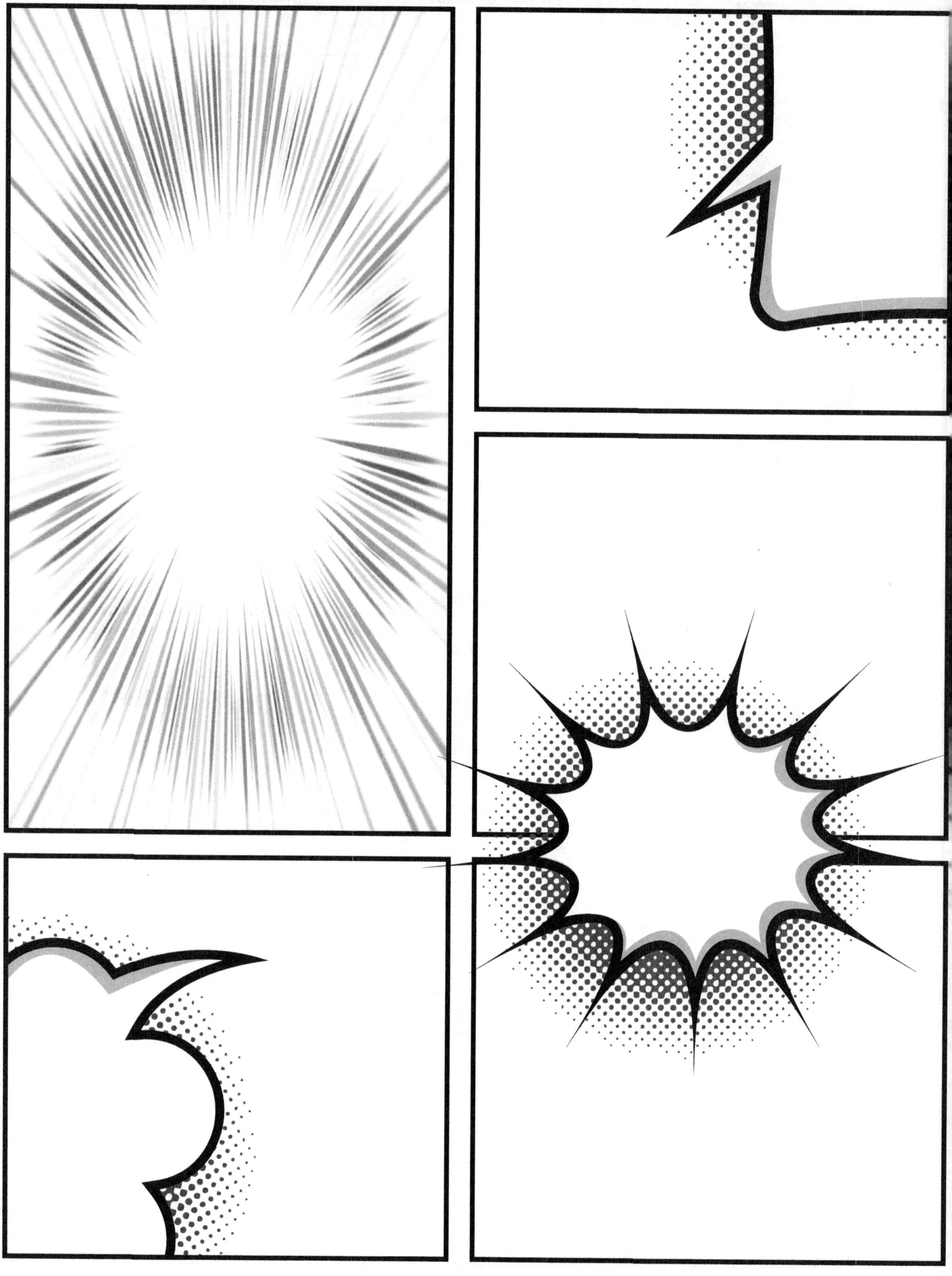

BOOM

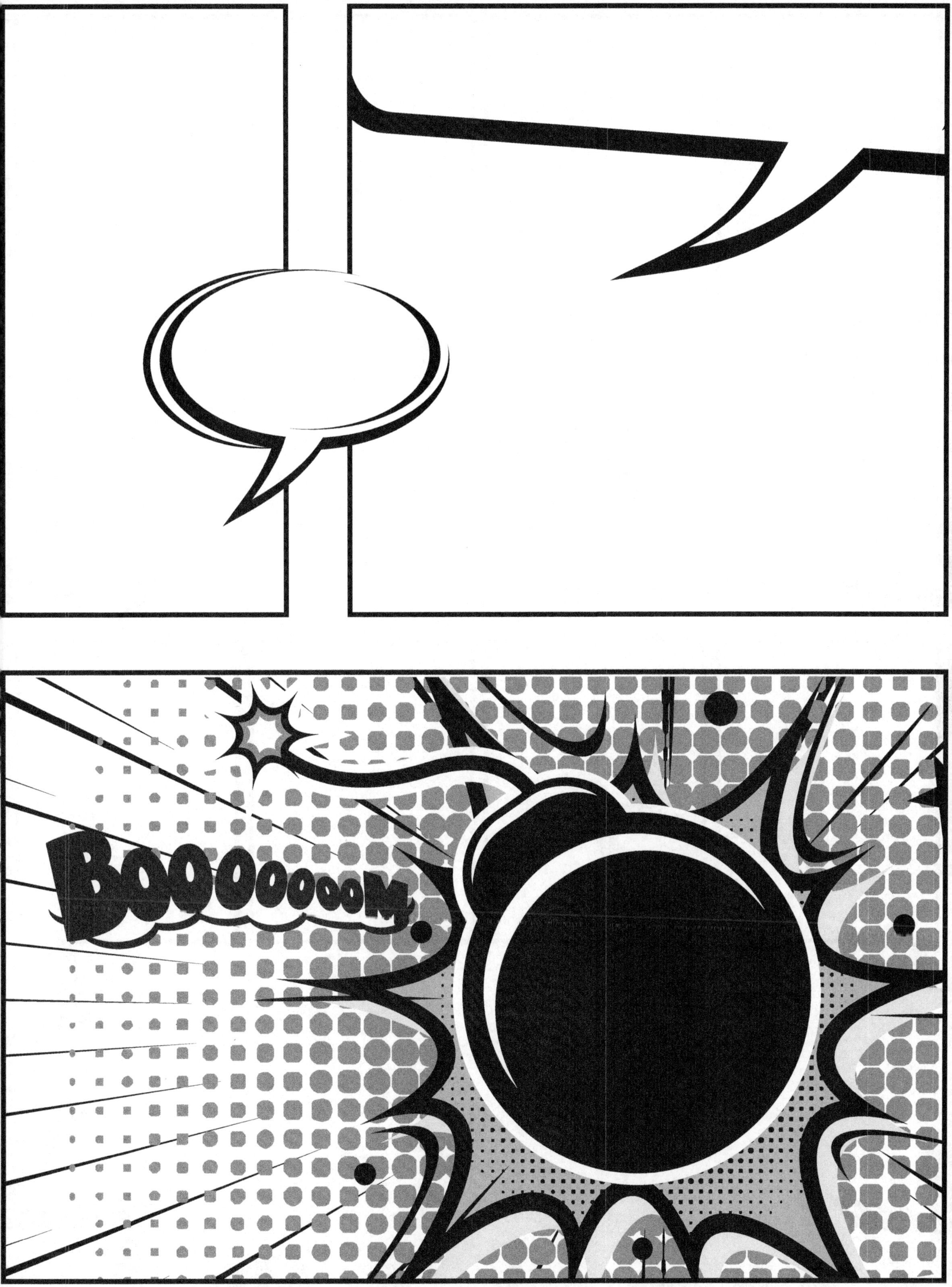
BOOOOOOOM

POW

BOOM

BANG
???

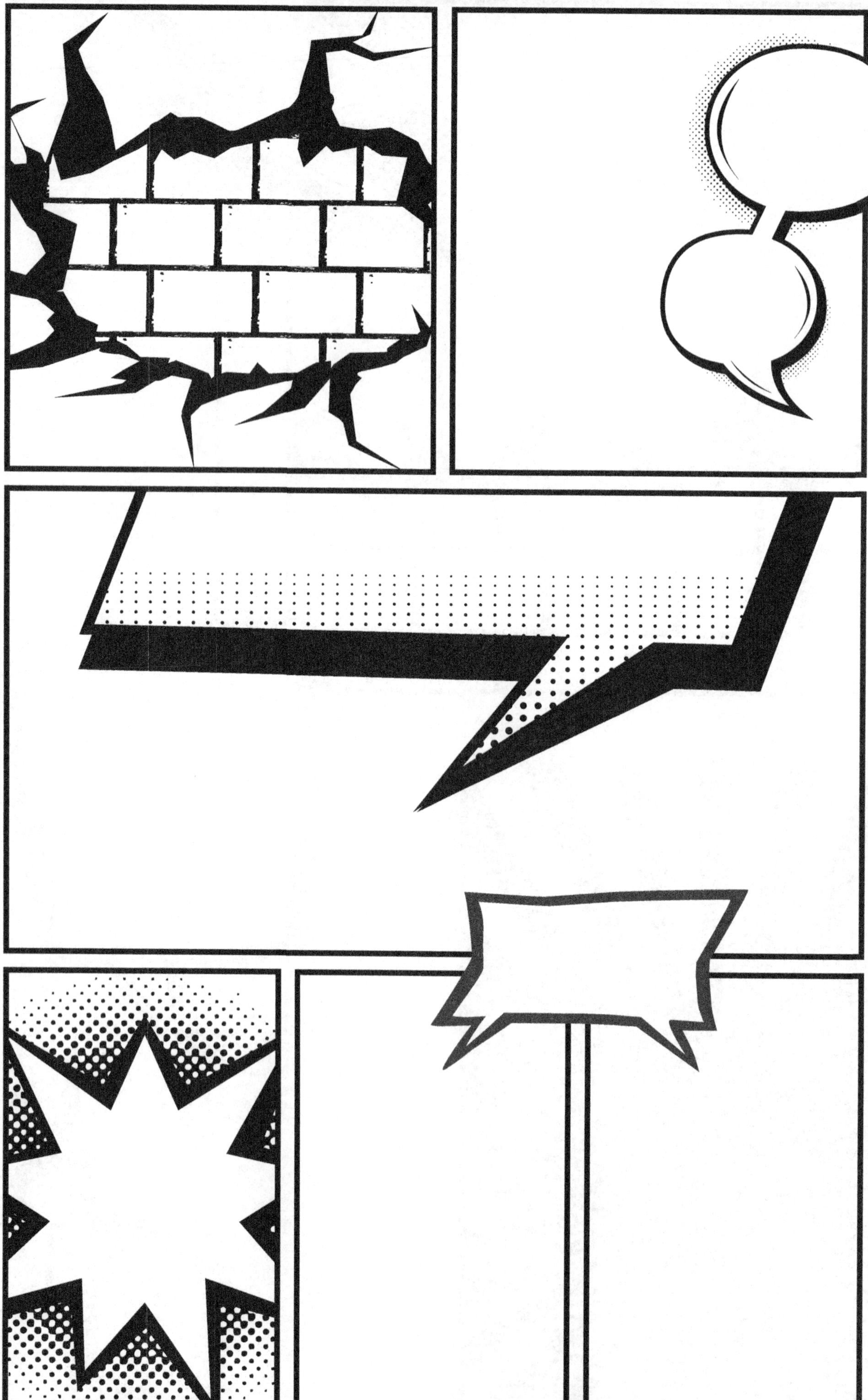

POW

CLANS

ZAP

ZWOSH!

CRUNCH!!

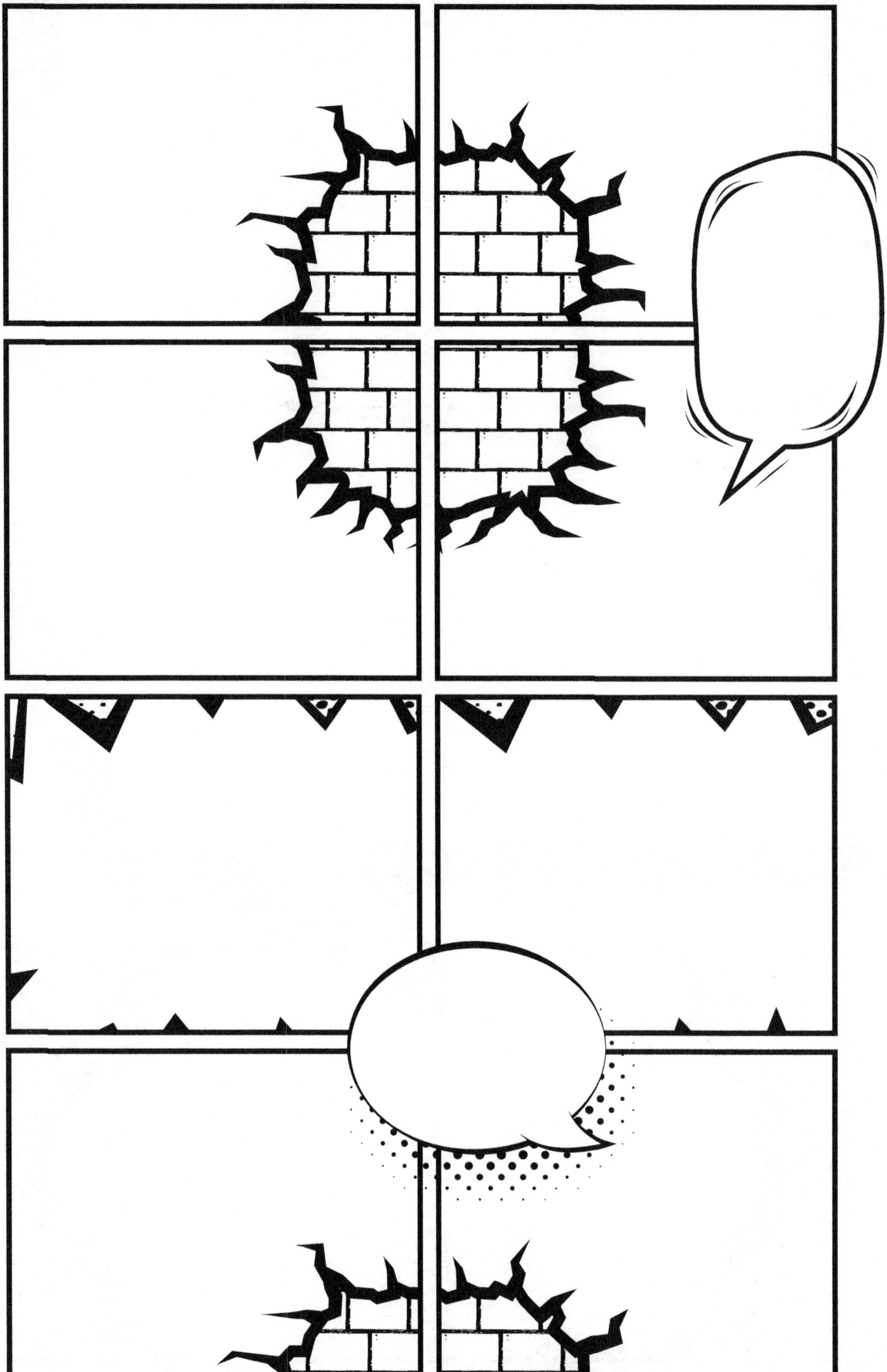

POW POW

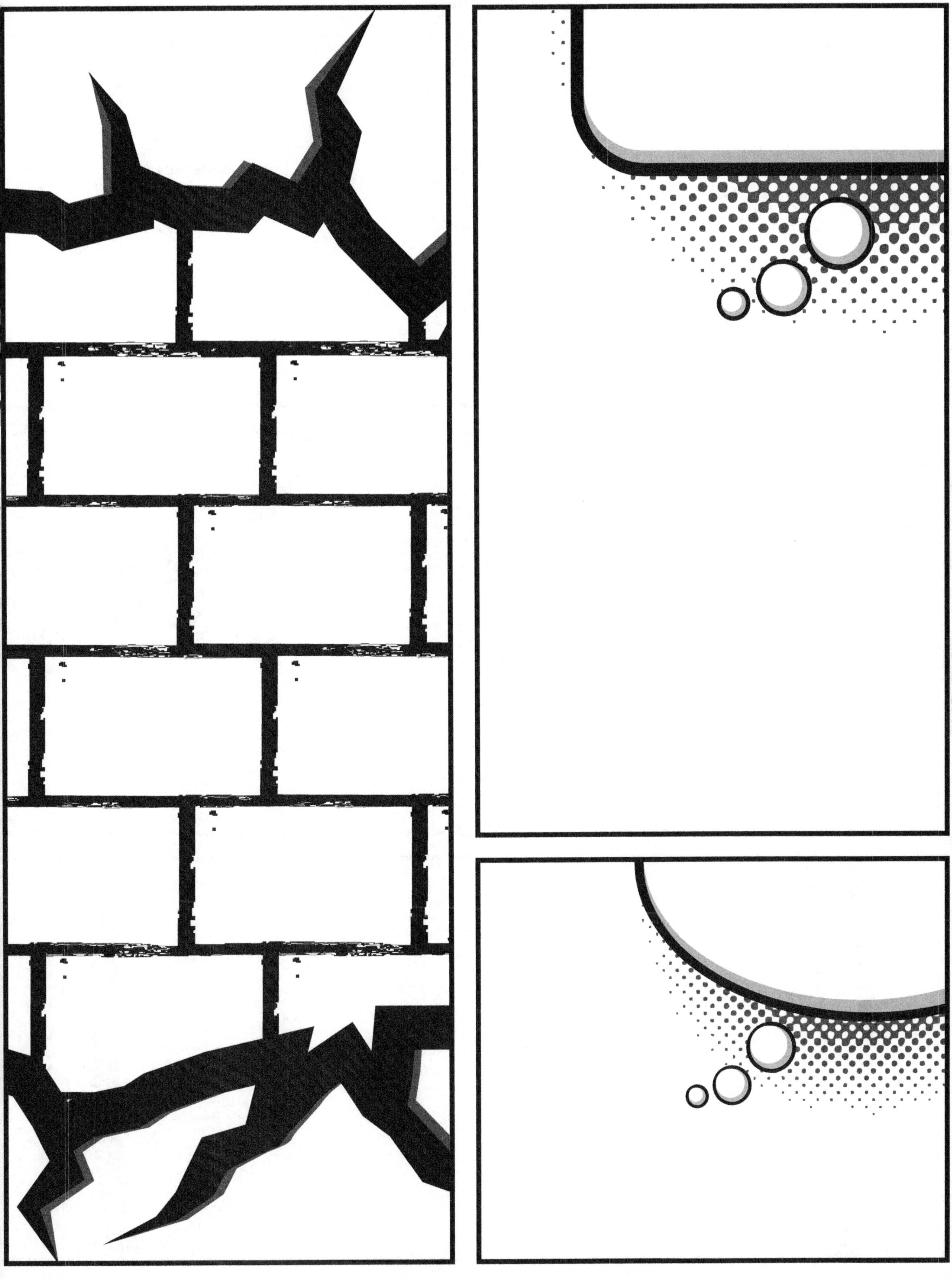

BOOOOOOM

Printed by Amazon Italia Logistica S.r.l.
Torrazza Piemonte (TO), Italy

54805921R00060